Breathwork

Now, the world is full of information on all the things we aren't doing right. It's sort of amazing that I am alive to write this and you are alive to read it with all the wrongness that social media accuses us of. So please don't take this as a "you've been breathing all wrong cuz you're dumb!" zine.

But we aren't breathing great. Because modern living doesn't account for the necessity of it. And we aren't taught it early on the way people in many other cultures are. Breathwork is really freaking important to both our physical and mental health. That is, managing our own body's reactions to stress and trauma and the toxic crap we breathe in all the time. You can geek out over the nervous system and polyvagal theory in my book *Unfuck Your Body*. But the short version is that you want to have normal responses, not batshit ones (unless life is actually being batshit).

Breath (*pranayama*) just happens to be one of the eight limbs of yoga. Now, I super pinky-swear I am not trying to trick you into doing yoga if that's not your jam, but Patanjali[1] figured out in the 2nd Century BCE, way before "modern" science did, that breath is a good way to keep your body and mind healthy and connected.

Some of these exercises come with contraindications. Just like something being a whole food supplement or herb doesn't make it a good choice for your body and circumstances, some breathing techniques may also be a bad idea. But hey, other than that? Breathing is free and you are already doing it anyway, so you might as well get a little fancy.

---

1 The ancient Indian sage who is thought to have authored many sanskrit texts, including The Yoga Sutras.

This Is Your Brain on Breathing

Breathing is one of those things that we control with both our conscious and unconscious brain. The unconscious part is managed by the brainstem, which is the keeping-the-body-alive part of the brain. It's often called the reptilian brain, though it's more complicated than that in reality. An example is how the neural circuit in the brainstem affects the connection between breathing and brain control. That neural circuit is actually our "breathing pacemaker" because it adjusts itself based on alterations of our breathing rhythms.

If something activates our fight or flight response (like a big dog chasing us) our breathing will become faster and more erratic. Our heart rate goes up, our neural activity goes all kinds of wonky, and we have a strong emotional response, like anxiety, panic, fear, or anger. We all know that part, right? We've all lived that and some of us live it every day because of anxiety disorders that create imaginary big dogs on the regular. But here is the cool part; there is a bidirectional flow happening in this process.

Our experiences change our breathing, which changes our entire physiology. If we consciously change our breathing, we can also directly influence our physiology. Mindfully slowing our breathing increases our baroreflex sensitivity, which measures the amount of control over our own heart rate.

A recent study directly showed that changing our breathing can also change our emotions. If we control our breathing by counting breaths, we are influencing *neuronal oscillations* (super fancy way of saying brain waves if you are at a MENSA convention or looking to bore your Tinder date to death) throughout the brain, especially in the mid-brain regions that are related to the regulation of emotion.

And, according to a study in the journal of Cognition and Emotion, our breathing accounts for up to 40% of our emotional responses.

Controlling our breathing changes our vagal tone, triggering the parasympathetic nervous system which is the counterbalance of the "fight, flight, freeze" sympathetic nervous system response to stress (either real or perceived). This goes on to influence the entirety of our body and our long-term physical health (including activating the lymph nodes to better expel toxins), not just our short-term stress response.

Breathwork and Trauma Responses

Like any other intervention, those of us with trauma histories may need to take an extra special approach to breathwork.

I have over a decade of formal meditation practice and a pretty intense amount of clinical training in both breathwork and mindfulness. It can be (it *is*) still really difficult. I know. *I know.* Conscious alteration of your breathing when you are triggered or activated may feel completely undoable. Someone *telling* you how to do it feels even worse. So if you have had an awful experience in a meditation class or a yoga class, with a therapist, or listening to an app, you aren't the least bit crazy, that's really common. So I want to talk a little about why that is and how to plan for it.

Trauma changes our breathing. When we are out of our zone of tolerance, our breathing becomes shallow (to change oxygen movement throughout the body to prepare for the perceived attack). And trauma survivors often hold their breath regularly without realizing it. And that creates tension and more body dysregulation that we are often not even aware of.

We can learn from yoga practitioners who have been developing trauma-informed practices that can help us use mindful movement and breathing for trauma recovery, without being retraumatized or triggered by it. David Emerson's trauma-informed yoga is an evidence-based practice for trauma recovery, and there are several unique aspects to how he cues yoga that I use as a teacher and clinician.

One of the biggest differences in his approach is that he doesn't tell practitioners when to breathe in and out. He only suggests noticing it. If you have taken a more traditional yoga class, you'll remember being told when to breathe in and breathe out constantly. That's why the first breathwork exercise in this zine is designed to help you just *notice* your breath, with no plan of altering it. Trauma survivors regularly struggle to notice their breathing at all, so beginning to do so is a really big deal. And it helps us notice when we are holding our breath as well. While an anxiety or panic response can include very rapid, shallow breathing, a trauma response may invoke a locked jaw, breath suppression, and abdominal inhibition.

Another really amazing resource is David Treleaven's book *Trauma-Sensitive Mindfulness.* If you are a trauma survivor or an individual who works with trauma survivors, this book is invaluable. He offers suggestions for managing trauma triggers and activation during mindful meditation practice, which can also be applied to breathwork to help maintain that polyvagal window of tolerance:

- Recognize your internal *go* and *stop* signals (thoughts, feelings, body sensations) as markers of how you respond to different breathing techniques. Which are most helpful? Which are activating?
- Take breaks when you need to or alter how you are holding your body. Move into a more comfortable position or wiggle in place a little.

- Open your eyes, if they have been closed.
- Change to slow, mindful breathing if you were trying one of the more complicated pranayama techniques.
- Focus on an external object that is in your line of vision.
- Shorten your breathwork practice period or otherwise adjust the practice itself (for example, the 4-7-8 breathing pattern can be altered to shorter breaths).

Learn and practice breathwork when you are in a relaxed state, rather than trying to do it when you are already activated. The more you practice when your body isn't under siege, the more likely you are to be successful with it when your body *is* under siege.

Breathing Exercises

We're gonna start with the classic breathwork techniques, then move into some more specific

pranayama techniques, focusing on the ones that my clients have reported to be the most helpful over the years. I'm not just including pranayama because I'm a yoga dork. The impact of different pranayama techniques on physical and emotional health has been studied extensively in recent years.

Pranayama is the combination of three Sanskrit words: *prana* is our life force energy, *ayama* refers to lengthening and extending, and *yama* refers to containing or restricting.

This kind of breathwork is part of yoga, even though it's not what most of us think of when we hear that word. When we think of yoga, we think of the bendy shit. But the poses and forms, which are known in sanskrit as the *asanas,* are in fact only one of the eight limbs of yoga. Pranayama is another one of the eight. Many yoga practitioners will attest to the fact that pranayama is foundational to the asanas and the *dhyana* (meditation).

Pranayama is how we clear and cleanse our bodies, and the asanas and dhyana are how we test the efficacy of our breathing practice. And this is why the mindfulness and the bendy shit can be so difficult if you haven't gotten a handle on the breathing part.

A precaution about all of these techniques: If you have nose or throat irritation or congestion, it may not be a great breathwork day for you. If you have a strong negative response to any of the techniques, stop doing them immediately. Any specific contraindications for any technique will be listed in italics following the technique itself.

Noticing the Breath

Settle your body into a comfortable position. You can close your eyes if you feel comfortable doing so, or settle into a soft gaze instead.

Bring your awareness to your breathing. Notice as you breathe in, and follow through as you breathe out. When your thoughts wander, just notice them, maybe label them as "thinking," and bring your attention back to the breath. You can use Thich Naht Hahn's breathing mindfulness technique to help center your focus on being mindful in the moment:

Breathing in, I know I am breathing in…

Breathing out, I know I am breathing out.

Breathing in… I know I am breathing in…

Breathing out… I know I am breathing out…

Notice the rhythm of your breathing, notice how it changes. Notice the sensations in the rest of your body and how they change. Don't do anything to alter your breathing or to "breathe better," just pay attention to where you are now.

No specific contraindications.

Three-part Breathing

We've all done a big inhale before starting a new task, right? The inhale is our sympathetic nervous system becoming activated, which gives us an energy boost to act. Someone in distress is breathing so rapidly they are constantly inhaling, building up an energy flow that tells the brain to become anxious or panic.

The exhale is the parasympathetic response, which lowers our heart rate and calms our energy.

The retention (the space between inhale and exhale) is the space where we connect with our body and what's going on inside it (interoception). So the 4-7-8 breathing pattern is designed to manage a stress response by lengthening out our periods of interoception and parasympathetic engagement.

- Breathe in for a count of 4
- Hold for a count of 7
- And out for a count of 8

You may feel a little light headed at first, and it's totally okay to sit or lie down. Another option is to use the same ratio, but shorten it:

- Breathe in for a count of 2
- Hold for a count of 3.5

- And out for a count of 4

No specific contraindications.

The Complete Breath (Dirgha Pranayama)

Dirgha is a good daily practice to help manage breathing errors that we have collected over time. While you don't (and really can't) breathe like this 24/7, practicing with it daily will help you naturally lengthen, deepen, and relax your "regular" breathing.

- Get in a comfortable position—seated is best for this practice. Hold your spine as straight as you are comfortably able to, and let your abdomen soften.

- Place your hands on your abdomen, or bring awareness to that area. Gradually start to lengthen and deepen your breathing. Work to expand your belly like a balloon with each inhale, and deflate it back out upon exhale. This is abdominal (or belly) breathing.

- Now shift your attention to your ribcage. If you are able to place your hands on the side of your ribcage, do so and focus your breathing into that space. Feel the flexibility of your ribs as you expand them on inhale and relax them on exhale.

- Now shift your attention to your upper chest. If you are able to, place the tips of your fingers on the front of your chest right below the collar bone. Focus breathing into this area, bringing awareness to your chest lifting slightly upon inhale, and softening back into your body on exhale.

- Try combining all three parts. Exhale fully, then focus on inhaling into the belly, up through the ribcage, and then through the upper lungs. Gradually release the breath, noticing how the upper lungs, rib cage, and belly deflate as you do so.

Don't do Dirgha if you've had recent abdominal surgery, or if you have throat or sinus irritation or a respiratory infection.

Alternate Nostril Exercise (Nadi Shodhana Pranayama)
This technique is great for balancing the left and right hemispheres of the brain and balancing the vagal system. Studies of pranayama have demonstrated that alternate nostril breathing was the only type of breath work that was found to have a positive effect on the cardiovascular system (heart rate, respiratory rate, and blood pressure).

This breathing exercise involves breathing from alternate nostrils. This exercise cleans nostrils and sinuses. It is also helpful in the simultaneous activation of the left and right side of the brain.

- Get your body comfortable, sitting if possible.

- Place your left hand on your left knee, and lift your right hand up to your nose.

- Tuck your middle three fingers into the palm of your hand, leaving your pinky and thumb extended (the universal sign for "call me!")

- Complete an exhale, then use your right thumb to close your right nostril. Inhale through your left nostril.

- Use your pinky to close your left nostril while opening your right nostril and exhaling through the right nostril.

- That is one complete breath cycle. Continue for up to five minutes, making sure that you always finish your practice by finishing with an exhale on the left side.

Don't do alternate breathing if you have hypertension, an active migraine, or an active sinus or chest infection. Also generally be aware of discomfort if you have a full stomach.

Bee Breath (Bhramari Pranayama)

This technique has been shown to reduce stress and anger, help with sleep induction, and helps strengthen the muscles of the throat.

- Get comfortable, sitting upright if possible.
- Take a full inhalation
- Hold for three seconds,
- Close your ears using your index fingers
- Make a soft humming sound on exhale (like the sound of a buzzing honeybee).
- Repeat 5-6 times if possible.

As an alternative to closing your ears, you can place your thumb on the cartilage between your cheeks and your ears, so you feel the vibration but aren't blocking off your hearing.

Don't do bee breath if you are actively suffering from a migraine. Also generally be aware of discomfort if you have a full stomach.

Ocean Sounding Breath (Ujjaji Breathing)

This technique is fantastic for centering and focusing concentration without the nervous system activation that usually comes along with increasing our attention.

- Sit comfortably, upright if possible.
- Relax your jaw and keep your lips closed.
- Start with some deep breathing to bring your body's focus back to breathwork.
- Now softly contract the back of your throat so you are making a "hhhhhhhh" sound upon inhale and exhale. Think of how you would use your throat to fog up a mirror. It can also be helpful to hold your cupped hands in front of your mouth and breathe into them so it sounds like holding a seashell up to your ear.

If it's hard to hear yourself, some people do well using headphones to block out other noise so they can hear the sound from inside their head. It's much easier to create the ocean sounding breath on exhale than inhale, so focus on exhale first if it's taking you a while to get this technique down.

No specific contraindications.

Bubble Breathing

This breathing technique is specifically designed for individuals who really struggle with slow and deep breathing. Pursed lip breathing increases pressure on our airways in a good way... It helps them stay open long enough to exhale out stale air and possible toxins, which means we can take in more freshly inhaled air, leading to better circulation in our entire respiratory system. And since it is difficult to know if we are "doing it right," we can just blow bubbles.

Bubbles are super inexpensive, or can be DIY'd very easily (recipe for bubble juice and ideas for bubble wands listed below). Blowing bubbles, especially trying to blow the biggest bubbles we can, slows our breathing and naturally has us use pursed lip breathing.

- Take a long deep breath (so you have enough air to make a big bubble)
- Purse your lips and blow as slowly as possible to create the biggest bubble possible.

Homemade bubble solution:

- 1/2 cup dish soap
- 1 ½ cups water
- 2 teaspoons sugar

Mix well to blend and that's it!

Homemade bubble wand possibilities:

- Pipe cleaners bent to give you a loop and a handle
- Plastic funnels and drinking straws will work without modification
- Plastic cups or drink bottles can be used by cutting the bottom off the bottle and dipping it into the bubble solution.

This breathing technique has been tied to decreasing the efficacy of blood glucose-lowering medication so if you are on insulin or the like, talk to your doctor before trying it.